BE THE FIRST YOU

SNEHA JAIN

Made with ♥ on the Notion Press Platform
www.notionpress.com

"

To the self, who decided to be the first ME."

Contents

Contents

CHAPTER ONE

THE SENSE OF SELF

A person might often feel a constant nagging voice in his or her head which is nothing but the persistent inner critic saying out loud about how you cannot or will not be able to perform certain tasks successfully.At times, it is your own voice reminding yourself "This is me" or "This is not me". This is a very basic explanation for the concept of self. Your sense of self deals with knowng qualities about your own self like your values,convictions,wants,need,desires,principles and more.

BUILDING A STRONG SENSE OF SELF

The most common trait of a person with low sense of self is looking upto other people to make decisons on their behalf.

Begin by making choices for yourself and distinguishing yourself by figuring out your beliefs, values and truths apart from people's opinions.

A person might often feel a constant nagging voice in his or her head which is nothing but the persistent inner critic saying out loud about how you cannot or will not be able to perform certain tasks successfully .At times, it is your own voice reminding yourself "This is me" or "This is not me". This is a very basic explanation for the concept of self. Your sense of self deals with knowing qualities about your own self like your values, convictions ,wants, need, desires, principles and more.

BUILDING A STRONG SENSE OF SELF

The most common trait of a person with low sense of self is looking upto other people to make decisions on their behalf.

Begin by making choices for yourself and distinguishing yourself by figuring out your beliefs, values and truths apart from people's opinions.

It is truly said that our ideal self is the self we aspire to be. If the way we are, that is our real self, is aligned with the way we aspire to be, then we feel a sense of mental well-being and peace of mind.

Ever wondered if you are the same person when you were four, eight or twelve?

In some way you might be the same while , at the same time, you might be different in many factors.

Learn to be alright while being alone, set boundaries and do things for yourself. Quit fawning, practice yoga ,listen to music or perform your favourite activity. In other words, introspect yourself and know your own real self better.

"Instead of waiting for approval from others ,learn to identify yourself without looking into the mirror."

LET US NOW KNOW THE LEVEL OF OUR SENSE OF SELF

What do I value most?

Where do my values come from?

Are there aspects of my behavior that I could improve upon?

How do I define success? Why is success important to me?

What are my strengths?

What does "a good life" look like to me?

What am I ashamed of? Why?

Am I trying to move past painful experiences? Am I dwelling? Avoiding?

What are my weaknesses?

CHAPTER TWO

VISION

The moment we hear the word "vision" we interpret the meaning to be something related to seeing. Indeed, vision is the view or idea of what something could be in the future. Your dreams need a vision to be fulfilled. The harsh reality is that if you do not develop your own vision, you will allow other people and circumstances to direct the course of your life. Think of crafting your life vision as mapping a path to your personal and professional dreams. Life satisfaction and personal happiness are within reach. Creating a vision for your life might seem like a frivolous, fantastical waste of time, but it's not: creating a compelling vision of the life you want is actually one of the most effective strategies for achieving the life of your dreams.

WHY VISION?

In this world, there is nothing more than just blindly following the crowd and not worrying about whether the path you are following is correct or not.

Having a vision in life has its own perks. It not only gives you a purpose but also makes all your hard work worthwhile, for you are well aware of the path you follow.When you have a vision, you try to find your own solutions whenever you are stuck somewhere. It makes you wiser every time and affects your personality in a very positive way. Your level of maturity rises and sense of responsibility improves.

It is difficult to arrive at the vision(s) without having the clarity of purpose of your life you get to choose and refine as you go. Again, here, the purpose of your life is aligned to who you are, your surrounding, context, your beliefs, values, and the meanings you attach to yourself and your life around and ahead.

Once you know your purpose, vision is a visualization of how that purpose gets accomplished. This visualization has a positioning, benchmark and clarity as to the characteristics.

Finally, commit time, energy and resources to the Life Vision you created, even though you may have no idea how or when it will come true. Set the intention, be patient and make at least a small step every day in the direction of your Life Vision.

" Your life vision acts as a magnet to your accomplishments"

HOW STRONG IS OUR VISION?

What is my burning passion, what am I truly passionate about?

How will my work, career or business enable me to live those dreams?

If I could invent the future, what would I create for myself?

What would my ideal or perfect day look like?

If I had a magic wand and could change any one thing about my life, what would I change?

If I knew failure wasn't an option, what would I attempt to achieve or do with my life?

What mission in life absolutely inspires me?

What work do I find absorbing, engaging and truly enjoy?

If someone were to describe me, what words would I want them to use?

CHAPTER THREE

FOCUS

Just like everyone else on this planet, you deserve to get what you want out of life.

Already wondering about why to focus on myself?That doesn't mean you're a selfish person; it simply means you're the one who has to work for it. Modern life is full of distracting clamor, from text messages and emails to window displays in the mall. Other people tug at you with their priorities — which may not be your own. And it can feel scary to admit what really matters to you, tell others, and go after it for real: the fearful voices whisper in the back of the mind: What if you fail?

If you do not prioritize things that are the most important to you, they might get overrun by the bermudagrass of less important priorities.

Knowing your purpose in life should be the most important aspect of your life. If you ever communicate about your purpose in life then do so with self-respect, not self - doubt.

Clarifying the priorities would certainly help you to practically look onto a particular priority with the importance factor. As the saying goes "Put the bigger rocks in the bucket first", focus on your most important priority first. Also see what realistic changes you can gradually make in your time, in the people you see, in what you give your attention, in how you spend your money. Build your priorities into your daily schedule and monthly budget.

Most of us have a daily routine, with many fixed activities and chores. Evaluate which things are absolutely necessary and important for the five areas you identified as having the most value for your life. What would you do with all the time you would have available if much of the daily activities were radically decreased or curtailed?

Periodically get rid of emotional and psychological clutter, those ways of being that no longer serve you. Too often, we continue to do things routinely, often in a way that has little to do with how we have evolved over the course of time. We need to let old things go in order to make room for the new things and ways of being that truly reflect who we are and where we are.

"When you focus on something, the irrelevant surroundings do get blurred"

SWOC Test

Get a sheet of paper and create a 2X2 grid. This will give you four cells, which are to be labeled as Strengths, Weaknesses, Opportunities, and Challenges.

Think about yourself and your life, and then under Strengths, list everything you are good at and the significant resources that you have. As you do so, remember that being a part of God and one with God is a phenomenal strength. Your knowledge, talents, and network of family and friends are also strengths.

Under Weaknesses, list your areas for improvement. We all have areas for improvement in ourselves and our lives. If you are not sure what areas you need to improve, you can ask someone who you believe will tell you the truth. Sometimes it is easier to identify areas for improvement in others than it is to identify them for ourselves. You can ask the person to help you identify your strengths as well as your areas for improvement. As you do your SWOC, focus on the major areas for improvement and those that will help you live a better life.

Under Opportunities, list the things you think you can do to improve yourself and your life, your options in life, and things you believe are possible for you. Think about new things you can do, things that can be done differently and better, and keep an open mind.

Under Challenges, list some of the major difficulties you are experiencing, the obstacles you face, and any major threat in your life. As you list your strengths, weaknesses, opportunities, and challenges, also include political issues, economic factors, social issues, technology, legal issues, and environmental issues that affect you. Think also about your spirituality, health, finances, family, friends, relationships, job, career, business, personal development, love, peace, joy, how much you are truly enjoying your life, and other important aspects.

After identifying your strengths, weakness, opportunities and challenges, ask yourself the following questions:

1.How can I use my strengths to help myself, serve others, and live a better life?

2.Which of my weaknesses do I need to improve, and how can I improve them?

3.What opportunities can I explore to improve myself and my life?

4.What can I do about the challenges I face?

CHAPTER FOUR

PASSION

Each one of us, at some point in time, think to ourselves, What is my passion in life? Finding passion is never easy. Many people spend their entire lives finding out what they truly want in life. It is very arduous to identify your passion in life.

Yet the power of your passion is so incredible that it could change your entire life. Without your passion the chances are you will live a life of mediocrity. That is why it is so important for you to discover where your passion lies.Passion may be a bit tricky to define, but we all recognize it when we see it, whether in ourselves or in others. Passion is what gives you boundless energy, intense almost single-minded focus and the willpower to overcome even the most daunting obstacles.

Life sometimes has a way of pulling us away from things we once loved. Ask yourself "What was my passion in years past?" If you're searching for your passion, it may be that you feel you've lost some spark along the way. Taking time out for some personal restoration can be a valuable first step on the path to reigniting your passion.The old saying has it that if you do what you love, you'll never work a day in your life. But realistically speaking, not every career or business is driven by a deep-seated passion. Plenty of people work as practical necessity without especially loving what they're doing.

Regardless of whatever a person considers a success, he has to have a drive to achieve it. Normally, a person pursues what he is passionate about and that is one way of making him fulfilled and contented, hence, a relative success to him. One of the importance of passion in achieving success is that it will make a person committed toward attaining that goal, no matter how hard the obstacles that will come his way. There is no easy way towards success.

Again, passion is contagious. If he is the one who is less interested about it, he should let himself be influenced why passionate people around him.A person might be contended doing things other than what he is passionate about, finding and doing his passion is priceless. Passion is fuel to one's life. Surely, one's endeavor becomes tough along the way.

"Passion is the main highway leading to the destination of success"

KNOW YOUR PASSION

What are you most passionately curious about, and fascinated by? What do you love to study and research, write about, blog about, investigate and try to understand?

Having a feel for what wants to emerge in any given situation—a conversation, a relationship, a career, a life—is a valuable skill in living fully. What do you sense is trying to emerge in your life at this juncture? What's trying to happen, to come to fruition?

Which, if any, of your involvements and activities typically make you feel like you're in a flow state?

Name some profound and affirmative personal change you could make (or perhaps should make) that even if it didn't heal your body, would still have a profound healing effect on your life.

Among the most consistent precursors of what are called "spontaneous remissions" from disease, is a profound and affirmative personal change just prior to the remission. It could be a revelatory experience, a reconciliation with a long-despised parent, the radical assumption of responsibility for your own life, a significant confession or admission, allowing a long-buried and essential part of you to finally emerge and be expressed, or the pursuit of a long-denied passion.

Name a few of the activities and involvements in your life where your energies tend to drain out, that take vitality from you rather than give it. Socializing out of guilt or obligation, Driving in rush hour traffic when you don't have to, television, letting yourself be trapped in conversations by talkaholics, digital busywork.

You're standing at a crossroads. There's a signpost in front of you with two signs on it, pointing in different directions. Without thinking too much, what's written on each of the signs (a word or short phrase)?

CHAPTER FIVE

AMBITION

What is the difference between animals and human beings? Animals don't have a purpose to live life. They just chase their fundamental needs such as food, water, sleep etc. But we humans have a choice to set an aim in life. This aim will drive us to keep running in life otherwise life will become meaningless.

Instead of dwelling on other people's accomplishments, you should concentrate on advancing your own life and career. You should view yourself as your most significant rival. When you put yourself in an environment filled with driven individuals, you may be more motivated to pursue your own goals.Allow yourself the opportunity to investigate several new avenues. Even if you are careless and make a few blunders along the road, this can still be a valuable part of the learning process.When developing your plans for the future, you should also use your imagination. You can always begin by setting ambitious objectives for yourself and then work backward to make them more achievable.

Ambition should not turn into day-dreams. Nobody can build castles in air. Only an idle man can do it. It is therefore advisable to be practical in your ambition. It also connotes an individual's desire to improve one's current life circumstances.

There is a belief that man's desires are never-ending. After completing one, another one crops up. It is just normal to aim for professional and personal developments in life. Surely, we all want the best of both worlds. Being successful in the professional field may not be as sweet when there is no one to share the success with, thus, we all ambition to have a loving family to come home to at night.

While there are people who have successfully attained their objectives in life, there are still those who failed to achieve their goals. Sometimes, the reason is that the individual did not stick to his or her goals. When making up one's mind on how to achieve a goal, individuals should never look at obstacles and hardships as a roadblock. Instead, they must consider it as a tower that they must overcome in order to enjoy the fruits of their labor.

Obtaining one's ambition is sometimes a risky endeavor, but only through planning and executing the plans, can one really understand and appreciate the talents one has. Nevertheless, without acting on the fulfillment of one's ambition, dreaming and wishing to become great is nothing.

"Either be ambitious enough to achieve

what you think is yours or be happy seeing anyone else attain it."

ARE WE AMBITIOUS ENOUGH?

Give an example of an important goal that you set in the past. Talk about your success in reaching it.

Describe a time when you made a suggestion to improve the work in your organization/department. What was the final outcome of your proposed change?

Where do you see yourself in five years?

What are the important goals you achieved this year?

CHAPTER SIX

WILLPOWER

Willpower goes by many names: drive, determination, self-discipline, self-control, resolve. In simplest words, it is the mental ability to resist temptations, sometimes called urges, impulses, or bad habits, in order to meet long-term goals.Given a difficult task, if you have thoughts that it would not work, then that is what you will get versus someone who thought that it will work.

You do not need to be at the moon to check your willpower. It shows in your life every day. Today this world is full of information. No matter what your profession is you will find something new to learn. But we do not have enough time to learn everything so we skip. Now what matter is the importance of that thing and your willpower to learn.Do you remember anytime of your life when you were determined to do something and you did it?

Your values and decisions work in tandem, influencing each other while shaping the course your life takes. Understanding what drives your choices is your first step learning how to increase willpower. There is a domino effect that starts with your beliefs – the ideas you hold to be true. Your beliefs are shaped by your life experiences, culture, mentors, education and faith. These influences create a complex system of belief that inspires your values – what you hold as important. If you grew up in poverty with few resources, it's likely you'll come to value stability and autonomy. These values then shape your attitudes toward almost everything.

As you work to understand how to improve willpower, think of yourself as a sailboat, with willpower being the wind that propels you and strategy being the rudder that guides you. Your strategy centers on continual self-awareness – investigating your beliefs and being willing to tweak the ones that are not serving you.

If you want to succeed in life, you have to be willing to do hard things. What are you doing in your life right now that is really hard? Something that you don't feel like doing, but you do it anyway. You don't grow by doing things that are comfortable. You have to be willing to step outside of your comfort zone and stretch yourself.

Your willpower gets stronger the more that you flex it. Start small. As your self-control grows, you can integrate more hard things into your daily life. Over time, you will feel more focused, confident, and in control of your life. In this state of mind, results come naturally because you've conditioned yourself for success.

"Willpower is the elevator to success"

Time to test the willpower

You have to solve 10 math tests. The problem is that you hate math! What would you do?

It's time to clean your house! Can you?

Alarm clock rings to wake you up. It's 7 AM, time to get up. Easy for you?

You've made up your mind to abstain from eating sweets today. How's your progress?

Doctor prescribed you a medicine for coughing. It tastes disgusting! What would you do?

Yesterday you made a promises during arguing. Will you keep it?

What do think about people who don't return books to the library?

CHAPTER SEVEN

COURAGE

Successful people are courageous. They have learned to confront their fears. They take risks and act in the face of danger. Their courage has enabled them to overcome what holds most people back. Their courage makes them overcome their own limits while others crack under the pressure.Fear and confidence in relation to courage can determine the success of a courageous act or goal. They can be seen as the independent variables in courage, and their relationship can affect how we respond to fear. In addition, the confidence that is being discussed here is self-confidence; Confidence in knowing one's skills and abilities and being able determine when to fight a fear or when to flight it.

Being fearful is a powerful force that can lead to stagnation. In fact, if fear is not viewed correctly it can prevent you from achieving your goals and pursuing opportunities. Consequently, many people allow fear to keep them stuck in their comfort zone rather than flexing their courage muscles and trying something new in spite of the risks.

Too many times, people assume that you are either born courageous or you're not. And while it is true that some people could be more predisposed to displaying courage, that doesn't mean that all is lost for you. In fact, it's best to view courage as a muscle. And while some people might be born with more defined muscles than others, everyone has the ability to improve their courage muscles with the right training and practice.Additionally, knowing what you're good at helps boost your confidence, which makes it more likely you will take risks and be courageous. Likewise, when you're confident in your abilities, you're much more willing to go all-in when an opportunity presents itself.Many times, comparing the two extremes is all you need to move beyond your fears because most of the time, the worst thing that could happen is often minimal in comparison to what you could gain by acting.

Consequently, look for ways to reduce the stress in your life. In addition to taking care of yourself, look for ways to unwind and decompress. In some instances, that might mean taking a short vacation or some much-needed time off work. Everyone needs a break now and then. So, if you feel too overwhelmed with the thought of trying to be more courageous, it could be that you first need to reduce the stress in your life.Most people are afraid of failure, which often keeps them stagnate or stuck in the same place. In fact, the fear of failure can lead people to develop rigid standards.

"Have the muscle to lift all your goals"

How courageous are you?

Do you have the stomach to stand on a platform for a cause that is needed?

Do you have the faith to stand for your faith despite what others think or say?

Do you have what it takes to stand when others can't or won't?

Do you have the guts to speak up for the weak and defend those who lack?

Do you have the strength to protect and serve for the cause of freedom, safety, and liberty?

Do you have the drive to be where you say you will be, say what you need to say, and honor people by returning their calls, emails, or texts?

CHAPTER EIGHT

Successful people are pretty optimistic in nature. They see opportunities and challenges where others see only problems and difficulties. Their optimism enabled them to envision a better future. In fact, it was the very belief that they can affect positive changes that made them take responsibility for a better future. Without this deep conviction, it's less likely to take action.

Being optimistic about life is definitely one among the top 5 qualities one need to have to be successful in life. After all, how one can be successful if he does not believe he can do the best. Right? No matter what you are trying to do or already have started doing, always be optimistic about it. You may have to face some setbacks, even some major ones at times but you have to make sure that you still be confident, hopeful and should be very optimistic.

Optimists don't like to give up when faced with a problem. Optimism can help you get up and fight to reach your goals, regardless of your obstacles and challenges. When faced with a setback, optimistic people will look at the ways the situation can change in their favour. These people are less stressed because they see minor problems either as opportunities or as minor setbacks that can be easily overcome. Pessimistic people, on the other hand, focus on a problem rather than look for ways to overcome it.

The way you look at things in life can affect the way you live. When you surround yourself with a positive attitude and optimistic view, it can help you understand that no matter how big your problem looks like, in the end, it is just a small and easily manageable one. Keeping an optimistic mind-set can help you boost happiness and confidence and it can help you stay resilient in the face of your challenges. The importance of optimism in your life should not be ignored. No matter what setbacks you face, it is important to understand that having an optimistic mindset can help you recover from those setbacks.

"Negativity starts from your mind, heart and soul"

ARE YOU AN OPTIMIST?

Think of a negative incident that recently happened to you and answer the following questions.

Was the incident the result of:

1.Your inability

2.External factors

How did the incident make you feel?

What does this negative incident mean?

CHAPTER NINE

PERSISTENCE

The importance of persistence in life is defined as continuing to move on with whatever goal has been planned originally even though an external event or initial losses may have slowed down, or temporarily halt a person while the person is on the way towards achieving their goals. A person needs to keep his or her mind positive for the same. Staying positive can be difficult these days because all of us are so hung up on everything that is wrong with the world, we don't even realize that many of us are speaking and thinking focuses on what's wrong and what needs to be done about it, rather than what's right.

We all know how important setting goals is for achieving success in any endeavor, so take some time to figure out what it is you want. Remember, nothing important was every accomplished without adversity, setbacks and difficulties to contend with along the way. You cannot persevere; much less succeed, if you never try to accomplish something. So many of us procrastinate, fear failure or are too frozen in our tracks to take the first step towards achievement. But everything needs a first step. Do not fear the failure. Stay away from naysayers; instead seek advice from those experienced in your field of endeavor and those who want you to succeed. If things do not work out the way you hoped, then review the steps you took and the process you followed. Reevaluate by examining what went wrong and where.

The greatest feelings of accomplishment derive from knowing you've overcome obstacles and conquered adversities to achieve your goals. Your ultimate success will be exponentially more satisfying and fulfilling when you know what it took to get there.

"Continuous hard work is the demand of favorable results"

TESTING YOUR PERSISTENCE

Tell me about a project or task that you finished, despite numerous setbacks.

What is your proudest achievement?

Can you tell me about a conflict at work or school that made you feel frustrated?

Tell me about a time you received negative feedback from your elder. How did that make you feel?

"THE VISIONARY LIGHTS FROM A DARK MIND"

"SHE-THE WITHERED FLOWER"

"THE JEWELS OF ELEGANCE"

"THE WIND AND THE GRIT"

9 798888 834626

Printed by Libri Plureos GmbH in Hamburg,
Germany